P9-DBT-155

Tim Berners-Lee and the Development of the World Wide Web

Ann G. Gaines

Mitchell Lane
PUBLISHERS

PO Box 619
Bear, Delaware 19701

Unlocking the Secrets of Science

Profiling 20th Century Achievers in Science, Medicine, and Technology

Tim Berners-Lee and the Development of the World Wide Web

Library of Congress Cataloging-in-Publication Data
Gaines, Ann.
    Tim Berners-Lee and the developoment of the World Wide Web/Ann Gaines.
        p. cm —(Unlocking the secrets of science)
    Includes bibliographical references and index.
    Summary: Profiles the young Englishman who is credited with transforming the Internet, which had its origins in a defensive weapons plan, into the global information and communications system called the World Wide Web.
        1. Berners-Lee, Tim—Juvenile literature. 2. Telecommunications engineers—Great Britain—Biography—Juvenile literature. 3. Computer programmers—Great Britain—Biography—Juvenile literature. 4. World Wide Web—History—Juvenile literature. [1. Berners-Lee, Tim. 2. Computer programmers. 3. World Wide Web—History.] I. Title. II. Series.
    TK102.56.B47 G35 2001
    025.04—dc21   2001038373

ABOUT THE AUTHOR: Ann Graham Gaines holds graduate degrees in American Civilization and Library and Information Science from the University of Texas at Austin. She has been a freelance writer for 18 years, specializing in nonfiction for children. Some of her recent books include *Sammy Sosa* (Chelsea House) and *Britney Spears* (Mitchell Lane). She lives near Gonzales, Texas with her husband and their four children.

PHOTO CREDITS: p. 6 CERN; p. 9 Sam Ogden/Science Photo Library; p. 10 Globe Photos; p. 18 AP Photo; p. 24 MIT Photo by Donna Covenev; p. 28 Archive Photos; p. 34 CERN; pp. 38, 41 AP Photo.

PUBLISHER'S NOTE: In selecting those persons to be profiled in this series, we first attempted to identify the most notable accomplishments of the 20th century in science, medicine, and technology. When we were done, we noted a serious deficiency in the inclusion of women. For the greater part of the 20th century science, medicine, and technology were male-dominated fields. In many cases, the contributions of women went unrecognized. Women have tried for years to be included in these areas, and in many cases, women worked side by side with men who took credit for their ideas and discoveries. Even as we move forward into the 21st century, we find women still sadly underrepresented. It is not an oversight, therefore, that we profiled mostly male achievers. Information simply does not exist to include a fair selection of women.

Contents

Tim Berners-Lee is regarded as the inventor of the World Wide Web, the global information and communications system so many millions of people now use every day.

Chapter 1

From War to Peace

● ●

Many inventions originally intended for warlike purposes have evolved into peaceful uses. The German V-2 rockets that terrorized London, England during the final months of World War II gave birth to the massive Saturn rockets that landed the first men on the moon a quarter of a century later. Penicillin research and production was vastly accelerated because of all the wounded soldiers during World War II, and immediately began saving lives all over the world.

And in a similar way, Tim Berners-Lee, a young Englishman who was working in Switzerland, took a discarded weapon of the United States called the Internet and changed it into a tool for the benefit of mankind.

Berners-Lee was a member of a generation of young people who grew up when the entire population of the world lived in fear of a nuclear war between the two most powerful nations on earth. If such a war happened it would likely destroy the human race. Many of the children who grew up in that time became disciples of peace. They were filled with a sense that people could live in harmony together and settle their disputes without killing. Many of them eventually lived their adult lives working toward that goal.

Tim Berners-Lee is the kind of a person who was always interested in peace and getting people together to solve their problems, as this statement from an interview in *The World Wide Web Journal* reveals.

"I believe in democracy, in people governing themselves," he said. "My belief is that for society to work, every individual has to be involved on a number of different scales. Each individual has to look after themselves, typically their family, their work group, their town, their county—there are a number of different groups. Sometimes these nest, which tend to make life easier, sometimes they're disparate, clashing. Also every individual has to have a lookout for the planet."

In three months in the fall of 1989, Berners-Lee used the Internet, a discarded defensive weapon of the United States government and its system of sending information over telephone lines, and invented the World Wide Web. Today the World Wide Web exists in every country, reaching tens of millions of homes around the world. People have become friends with other people they will never visit because of it. People conduct business and do shopping without ever leaving their homes. Someday soon elections might be held on it. Every year, it seems, humans find new and better ways to communicate through it.

Berners-Lee remains humble today about his achievement. "I pieced it together as I pursued my regular work and personal life," he explains in his book *Weaving the Web*. "But many other people, most of them unknown, contributed essential ingredients, in much the same almost random fashion. A group of individuals holding a common dream and working together at a distance brought about a great change."

Tim Berners-Lee is a thoughtful man who thinks and writes about how people can live in harmony. He sees the World Wide Web as helping them to do so.

In August 1945, the United States dropped atomic bombs on Japan. This ended World War II, but a new conflict would soon arise. The Internet was first created as a military tool during the Cold War.

Chapter 2
The Origin of the Internet

● ●

When the United States dropped two atomic bombs on Japan in August, 1945, the absolute terror of the destruction forced the Japanese to surrender unconditionally. World War II was over.

But another form of conflict began almost immediately. Even though they had been allies during World War II in the fight against Germany and Japan, the US and the Union of Soviet Socialist Republics (USSR) distrusted each other deeply. The USSR was conducting its own atomic research during the war, and aided by several spies in the US program who passed on vital information, the Soviets held their first atomic bomb tests in 1949. Now there were two world powers that possessed atomic bombs that could be delivered by jet aircraft and soon after by unmanned rockets.

Neither nation had any defense against such a nuclear holocaust. Both nations tried to stockpile thousands of bombs of increasing destructive power to frighten the other. Each of these countries soon had the ability to drop enough atomic bombs on its enemies that the entire population of the world could be destroyed or horribly changed forever.

This period of time was known as the Cold War. While the US and USSR never fought each other directly during this period, for about fifty years the entire world lived in the fear of world-wide nuclear destruction that could be triggered by some conflict between the two great superpowers.

For example, the Cuban missile crisis in 1962 came very close to setting off a catastrophic nuclear war. The USSR had secretly installed nuclear missiles in Cuba that could reach many US cities. When a US spy plane came back with photographs that revealed the existence of those missiles, President John F. Kennedy and his advisors demanded that they be removed. For several tense days, the world waited anxiously before the Soviets began to dismantle their missiles and the crisis ended.

By that time during the Cold War, the United States government had done many things to prepare for an attack with atomic bombs. They encouraged families to build bomb shelters in their homes. Children in schools were instructed to kneel underneath their desks with their hands covering the backs of their necks in the case of a nuclear attack. The government constructed many of the major interstate highways that exist in the country today to be able to evacuate major portions of the populations of cities that were targeted for a nuclear attack.

On October 15, 1957, the Soviets became the first nation to launch a satellite into orbit around the earth. Named Sputnik, it weighed 184 pounds and was the size of a basketball. The entire scientific community of the United States was shocked to find that the Soviets were ahead of them in what was quickly named the "space race." They feared that control of outer space would give the Soviets a superior position from which to deliver atomic weapons upon the United States.

It was crucial that the most important scientific and military people and information survive such an attack. So soon after Sputnik was launched, the President of the United States, Dwight Eisenhower, put together a group of the best scientists in the country under the direction of the Department of Defense. This group was called the Advanced

Research Projects Agency (ARPA). It was their job to find a way for the military and scientific community to survive such an attack.

ARPA desired most of all to allow close communications between the country's leading scientists—who were located mostly at different universities around the country—and the Department of Defense in Washington, DC. In the case of a nuclear attack on the United States, most highways and telephone lines would be destroyed. It was important to find a way for the surviving scientists and other government officials to still be able to communicate with each other by linking their computers together.

ARPA officially funded the founding of a network of scientific computers, called ARPANET, in the fall and winter of 1969. Larry Roberts accepted the position of manager and architect of the new network. He wanted to connect all ARPA-sponsored computers directly over dial-up telephone lines, which were everywhere. If the lines between two cities, say New York and Philadelphia, were destroyed in an attack, it would probably be possible to re-route the communications to go through other cities such as Albany or Buffalo.

Scientific computers, however, worked with several different types of operating systems, so they could not communicate directly with each other. It was as if a person speaking Chinese was trying to communicate with another person who only spoke German.

But each of these large scientific computers was linked to a smaller gateway computer, and these had no problem communicating with each other. So it was decided to have the same kinds of small computers at each institution to act as gateways for their bigger scientific computers. It would be like having people who all spoke English talking together, then translating into Chinese and German. In that way, the bigger computers would be able to understand the information that had just been sent to them.

By September 1969, two gateway computers at the University of California at Los Angeles and Stanford University in Palo Alto, California were linked to each other. Soon another two computers were added, one at the University of Utah and the other at the University of California at Santa Barbara. This network of four computers marked the birth of ARPANET.

At that time there were two other kinds of networks that were important to the scientific and military community, satellite networking (SATNET) and packet radio. By the spring of 1973, it was decided to add these networks into ARPANET. There was one major problem in doing this. Neither the satellite nor radio network had any small gateway computers that could be used to communicate with the computers already linked to the ARPANET. That summer, Vinton Cerf and Robert Kahn, two employees of ARPA, submitted to the government a proposal called the "Protocol for Packet Network Intercommunication." This proposal described a new way for computers to send messages.

First the computer sending the message contacted the computer which would receive it and told it that a message was coming. Then the sending computer broke the message down into many small parts, each containing just a few words of the message. Each of these small parts of the message was enclosed in an electronic envelope called a packet. Each packet was numbered, addressed to the computer that would receive it, and sent out over the telephone lines. Any of the computers along the ARPANET that would receive the packet would read its address and send it along until it finally reached its destination. The packets could travel any number of different routes to their final destination. In a message from a computer in Los Angeles, California to another in New York, New York, some packets may go through Atlanta, Georgia and some through Mankato, Minnesota. Eventually, they all arrive at the destination and are put back into order to reveal the complete message.

The computer that was supposed to receive the message would count all of the packets as they came in, remove the envelope or packet from each part of the message, and reassemble each part to form the complete original message. If any packets were missing, the computer would notify the original sender and tell it to send the missing packets again.

It was a truly marvelous invention. The packets could travel over any route of connected computers to reach the final destination. If any parts of the message were lost, they could be sent over again. Called Transmission Control Protocol, or TCP, the system underwent its first test in July, 1977. A message originating in San Francisco, California, went to London, England and then back to the University of Southern California using SATNET, radio packets, and the ARPANET. Not one bit of information was lost.

The next year, 1978, TCP was divided into two parts. Transmission Control Protocol was used to split up the message into parts and put it into electronic packets, while a new system, Internet Protocol (IP), was used to address the packets and make sure that the entire message arrived at its destination. The system became known as TCP/IP. On January 1, 1983, every network on ARPANET converted from the old NCP, or Network Control Protocol, to TCP/IP. Beginning in 1983, TCP/IP gradually began to be used by all computer systems for network communication. This system is still in use today.

As the ARPANET grew during the 1980s, more and more people in the university communities around the country began to be aware of the new advantages of instant and free communication. As long as they could use TCP/IP, people could send personal messages back and forth to each other. These personal messages soon became known as e-mail, short for electronic mail. People stopped calling the system ARPANET and began calling it the "Internet," short for inter-network.

After 1983, the military portion of the ARPANET had been changed over to MILnet, a network exclusively used for military communication. During the 1980s, however, other large networks were established by other departments of the United States government. The National Science Foundation created its own network of five supercomputers, the NSFnet. They used the same standards as ARPANET and asked a group of universities in the state of Michigan to administer it. The National Institute of Health, NASA (the space program), and the Department of Energy also set up networks using supercomputers to store and send their information. They too became a part of the quickly growing Internet.

As the Internet grew, there were more and more computers on the system. Every one of them needed an address so that communications could be established between them. A system called the Domain Name System, or DNS, which was begun in 1981 and finished in 1984, resulted in the system still in use today. The ".com" or ".net" that ends all of the addresses on the World Wide Web today is a part of the Domain Name System.

In 1989, ARPANET went out of business when the United States government quietly stopped funding the project. The Internet itself hardly noticed and administration of the network was taken over by the National Science Foundation. The next year, 1990, the Department of Defense decided that all of the computers within its Department would quit using TCP/IP. They changed over to a system called OSI protocols.

By now, the Internet had reached a critical point in its development. The entire system had been designed as a defensive weapon in the Cold War, but by 1989, the United States government and its military had abandoned it in favor of a more exclusive, better protected system to link its computers. The Internet contained huge amounts of scientific data, but little else. The whole system was still difficult to use for anyone who was not a computer expert.

Then in 1989, a young British physicist named Tim Berners-Lee turned his mind to the problem. In just over two months, sitting at his desk in Geneva, Switzerland, he created a system to put a face on the Internet that would make it easier for anyone using the Internet to share any kind of information. His invention came to be called the World Wide Web.

At first, Tim Berners-Lee's invention of the World Wide Web was not well received. Although it took him several years of hard work to show others how wonderful it was, he was convinced of the potential of his system to join the entire world in one space where all of the world's knowledge and potential to solve problems would be available to everyone all of the time. It was a daunting vision.

Today Tim Berners-Lee heads up the World Wide Web Consortium, which coordinates Web developments around the world.

Chapter 3

Tim Berners-Lee

• •

Timothy J. Berners-Lee was born in London, England on June 8, 1955. His parents, Conway and Mary Berners-Lee, were both mathematicians. They worked together to help produce England's first commercial stored-program computer, the Manchester University "Mark I," which was sold by Ferranti Ltd. in the early 1950s.

Tim grew up during the Cold War in a neighborhood near London. The Berners-Lee family was quite friendly and close. They had their evening meals together and Tim and his younger brother Peter often discussed complex mathematical problems at the table together for fun, such as the square root of an imaginary number like -4.

Mary Berners-Lee gave the children a love and appreciation of life itself in the things she would do around the house. She hung cotton threads down into the bathtub so that spiders which had fallen inside could climb out before they were washed down the drain. Tim was taken to the local Anglican Church as a boy, but he has since become a Unitarian, a religion that stresses the fundamental need for people to be good to one another rather than religious ceremony.

As so often happens with children who are raised in a loving home, the young Berners-Lee wanted to be just like his parents when he grew up. He constructed a model of the Ferranti computer from cardboard boxes. It even had a make-believe clock and punch cards. In *Weaving the Web*, Berners-Lee recalled the family's early fascination with computers.

"My parents were full of excitement over the idea that, in principle, a person could program a computer to do almost anything," he said. "They also knew, however, that computers were good at logical organizing and processing, but not random associations. A computer typically keeps information in rigid hierarchies and matrices, whereas the human mind has the special ability to link random bits of data. When I smell coffee, strong and stale, I may find myself again in a small room over a corner coffeehouse in Oxford. My brain makes a link, and instantly transports me there."

During his youth, Berners-Lee read a lot of science fiction. He especially liked the works of Arthur C. Clarke, the science fiction writer who first described a system of communication satellites above the earth that were at an exact distance from the earth so that they would remain over the earth to constantly receive radio signals. There are thousands of such satellites now, and they are responsible for most of the instantaneous telephone and television systems that make us a global village today.

An Arthur C. Clarke story that really appealed to him was "Dial F for Frankenstein." This story is about computers and how computers are linked together to form a vast knowledge system that all of a sudden comes alive, just like Frankenstein. The computer system starts to breathe, to think, and to react on its own. How this super-intelligent computer Frankenstein reacted, for good or evil, was never discussed.

Berners-Lee attended the Emanuel School, a private boys' school in southwest London that had been founded in 1594, from 1969 to 1973. His younger brother, Peter, also attended Emanuel.

After leaving Emanuel, Berners-Lee attended Queens College at the University of Oxford where he studied physics. He chose physics because it combined the study of mathematics and electronics. He graduated in 1976 with first-class honors in theoretical physics.

"Physics was fun," he told Joshua Quittner in *Time* magazine.

While Berners-Lee was at Oxford he built his first real computer with a soldering iron, some simple electronic parts, an M6800 processor, and an old television set. "Building it gave me a great sense of adventure," he later said in an online interview with the computer chip manufacturer Intel.

"I bought one of the first kits to make your own personal computer in 1975," he remembered. "It was tremendous fun. It was great to be able to actually go and do whatever you like with a computer because a computer gives you the sense of unbounded possibility. And to be able to explore by yourself—unbounded by the constraints imposed by anybody else who has rules about what sort of language you should program it in—is a wonderful thing."

Berners-Lee's first job after college was with Plessey Telecommunications in Dorset, England, a major communications equipment manufacturer. He stayed two years with them, working on designing bar code technology and communications systems. In 1978, he joined the D.G. Nash company, also located in Dorset. There he wrote computer programs for typesetting machines used for printing books. He also designed and wrote the program for a computer system that could multitask—do several things at once.

Then, in 1980, he took a six-month contract as a computer programmer with the European Laboratory for

Particle Physics, known as CERN for its name in French, *Centre Européen de Recherche Nucléaire.* CERN—located near Geneva, Switzerland—was the world's most advanced laboratory for the study of the basic particles that make up everything in the universe. From all over the world, the best scientists would come to CERN to do experiments and exchange ideas. It was an exciting place to be for someone who found physics fun.

Daily life at CERN was quite hectic. Often scientists from many different countries would come and go. Every few weeks new people arrived. With names and ideas being tossed around every day in several languages, Berners-Lee found it hard to keep track of it all. He wrote a piece of software for his computer, a kind of notebook and address book that could keep track of all the random associations one comes across in real life and brains are supposed to be so good at remembering.

He had always been interested in the way that the brain works, and especially the way memories are stored in the brain. In *Weaving the Web*, he wrote that "One day when I came home from high school, I found my father working on a speech for Basil de Ferranti. He was reading books on the brain, looking for clues about how to make a computer intuitive, able to complete connections as the brain did. We discussed the point; then my father went on to his speech and I went on to my homework. But the idea stayed with me that computers could become much more powerful if they could be programmed to link otherwise unconnected information."

Berners-Lee called his new program "Enquire." When he was a boy, one of the thousands of books he read was an old one-volume English encyclopedia that he found in his home, named *Enquire Within Upon Everything.* The title captivated his imagination more than the thousands of old recipes and facts found in the book. Imagine the magic of a book that once opened revealed the answer to any question you may have!

Tim Berners-Lee first worked for CERN in 1980.

Chapter 4
"Enquire"

●●

The model that Tim Berners-Lee chose for Enquire was called "hypertext," a process first used by a scientist named Vannevar Bush in 1945. The term was used to describe a kind of writing that was possible on computers. A visible marker on a word or phrase would appear on the computer screen. When chosen by the reader by a mouse click or typing a number, another screen of writing, possibly about an entirely different subject, would now appear.

In his version of Enquire, Berners-Lee typed a page of information about a person, a device, or a program at CERN. The only way to write a new page was to link it to another page, or node. The links would show up as a numbered list at the bottom of each page, much like the footnotes in a book. The only way of finding information was to browse Enquire from the first page. It was quite basic and simple. The core idea of the program was to use a link in one document that would take the reader directly to another document. From that second document, the reader could link to a third document that was not linked to the first. Although Enquire only worked on the computer in Berners-Lee's office, it was a very powerful idea. Eventually, Enquire turned into a database of people and programs at CERN.

But nothing came of it because Berners-Lee left Enquire at CERN when his six months were up and he returned to private business in England. From 1981 until 1984, he worked at John Poole's Image Computer Systems Ltd., with technical design responsibility. His work included designing both the hardware and communications software to create superfast printing devices. He also wrote the computer language that was used to operate the entire system. In 1984, he began another fellowship at CERN, to work on distributed real-time systems for scientific data acquisition and system control.

Berners-Lee wrote the Enquire program again, this time designing it to run on all kinds of computers at CERN. In *Weaving the Web*, he said, "In addition to keeping track of relationships between all the people, experiments, and machines, I wanted to access different kinds of information, such as a researcher's technical papers, the manuals for different software modules, minutes of meetings, hastily scribbled notes, and so on. Furthermore, I found myself answering the same questions asked frequently of me by different people. It would be so much easier if everyone could just read my database."

He decided that the hypertext links that would be placed in the new Enquire would be shown by highlighting the appropriate word or phrase. It would appear darker on the screen, just as hypertext links are shown on the World Wide Web today.

There still remained the problem of how all of the different computers that were being used at CERN could call up hypertext links to pages throughout the Center. So he wrote a computer program called a "remote procedure call" that allowed a program on one computer on a network to run another computer on the same network, even if the computers used different languages. In this way, all the computers attached to the CERN cables would be able to use the same database, both the parts they already stored and the parts stored on other computers throughout CERN's many buildings.

He submitted his first proposal to link all of CERN's resources by hypertext to his bosses in March 1989. There was no response.

In truth, CERN was a physics research facility, which spent almost all of any available funds on new equipment and supplies for its scientists. There was little support for Berners-Lee's documentation system. Though the lack of response was disappointing, it became just another step on the way to getting a system up and running. Berners-Lee was not discouraged enough to abandon the idea.

He was aware of the Internet, which at that time was used only in the United States. So he talked with a fellow worker at CERN, Ben Segal, and the two men agreed that the TCP/IP system of communication that was used on the Internet should be used in the new version of Enquire.

TCP/IP allowed computers to communicate simply by hooking them into the already existing telephone lines. The scientists who worked at CERN and then returned to their home countries would be able to plug their computers into telephone lines at home and continue to receive and send information just as if they were still in Switzerland. Enquire would become a global system.

Berners-Lee started looking around for a new name for Enquire. He wanted a name that gave people the idea that it was a global document system that allowed anyone to establish a personal database and link it to anyone else's. He thought of "HT" for "hypertext." Another idea was "Infomesh," but that sounded too much like "infomess." Then he considered "The Information Mine," but its abbreviation was TIM. A modest man, Tim Berners-Lee thought that that made him sound too self-important.

Finally he decided on "World Wide Web."

Tim Berners-Lee works very hard to explain and promote the World Wide Web.

Chapter 5
The World Wide Web

• •

The new World Wide Web could use TCP/IP to send its information, but it simply could not exist in the same way as the Internet did. It still took an expert to use the Internet. One would run one program to connect to another computer, another program to communicate with a remote database, and still the data received from that remote location might not translate correctly on the home computer.

Berners-Lee wanted everyone in the world to be able to use the World Wide Web, not just computer experts. Gradually, the idea for and the possibilities of the new Web grew in his mind. He saw it as a way for everyone in the world to be able to work together to solve the common problems of humanity.

"The dream behind the Web is of a common information space in which we communicate by sharing information," he explained in an online biography on the World Wide Web Consortium webpage. "Its universality is essential: the fact that a hypertext link can point to anything, be it personal, local or global, be it draft or highly polished. There was a second part of the dream, too, dependent on the Web being so generally used that it became a realistic mirror of the ways in which we work and play and socialize. That was that once the state of our interactions was on line, we could then use computers to help us analyze it, make sense of what we are doing, where we individually fit in, and how we can better work together."

In October 1990, Berners-Lee began to create the parts of the World Wide Web on his own. He had recently received a new computer, a NeXT computer manufactured in the United States. It was a marvelous machine, well ahead of its time, and he took advantage of some of its advanced features to make a working model of the new World Wide Web.

The first thing that he did was to create what the World Wide Web would look like on the computer screen when the entire system was finished. He decided on a window that appeared in the middle of the screen to display the hypertext page. Around the window was a series of buttons, menus, and other choices that the reader could use to move around the World Wide Web. Today, we would call this first part of the web the browser. Berners-Lee called it the client program.

"The meat of it was creating the actual hypertext window," he said of this part of the project in *Weaving the Web*. It was nothing like the modern web browsers that can display graphic images, movies, stereo sound, and almost anything else. His primitive browser could display only simple text.

How were the various computers envisioned to take part in the new World Wide Web going to display the hypertext pages? All sorts of word processing software programs were being used on the computers around the world. There was no guarantee that a page could be received correctly by all of those on the web. So Berners-Lee wrote a fully functional word processing program that allowed the creation, browsing, and editing of the hypertext pages. He called this program the Hypertext Mark-Up Language, or HTML.

The next part of the World Wide Web that Tim put into place was the method by which the hypertext pages would be sent between computers. He invented the communication standard that he called the Hypertext Transfer Protocol, or HTTP. It was a computer software program that packaged the hypertext pages into a form that the packets of TCP/IP could deliver between machines and then reconstruct into machine-readable HTML form.

There already were several other sets of these rules, or "protocols," to transfer information over the Internet. The File Transfer Protocol (FTP) and Network News Transfer Protocol (NNTP) were communications protocols that were already in use on the Internet. There were technical difficulties—including the slow speed of these systems—that made Berners-Lee want to create a new one for the Web. Tim designed his system to retrieve a document quite quickly, in a tenth of a second or better. HTTP was quicker than the other systems, but would people want to switch over? Maybe not.

Berners-Lee had learned several lessons from the fate of the NeXT computer. Although it was well ahead of its time in its capabilities, few people bought the NeXT computer because, he felt, there were simply too many new features on the machine. It presented too great a learning curve for the average computer user to find comfortable. He wanted to keep as much of the new World Wide Web as familiar to everyone as he could. Where a change to existing conditions was necessary, he made sure that everyone's old standards and databases would work with the new system. In *Weaving the Web*, he remembers how he made HTTP acceptable to the old standards.

"The key to resolving this was the design of the URI," he said. "It is the most fundamental innovation of the Web, because it is the one specification that every Web program, client or server, anywhere uses when any link is followed."

All hyperlinks placed in a web page, indeed all web pages, have a unique address that Berners-Lee called a URI, or Universal Resource Identifier. This address is what the computer points to when the darkened hypertext link is chosen by the user. The computer then sends a message over the Internet to this address and asks the other computer to send that hypertext page.

Like regular postal addresses, a URI has several parts, which are separated by slashes. The computer program that displays the web pages knows how to recognize each part of the URI and act accordingly.

The first part of the URI identifies which protocol to use to send for data, such as "http:" or "ftp:" over the Internet. This first part is separated from the rest of the address by two slashes, such as "http://."

The next part of the URI identifies the computer somewhere in the world that contains the hypertext page. This part too is separated from the rest of the address by a slash. The final part of the URI is the identity of the desired page itself. A full URI could look like this: "http://www.the-cia.net/users/3dkids." The name has been changed today to URL, or Uniform Resource Locator, but the structure remains unchanged and is familiar to anyone who uses the World Wide Web today.

Berners-Lee was almost finished. He simply lacked any hypertext pages to display. He gathered all of his notes on how he put the World Wide Web together and put them on a separate part of the hard drive on his NeXT computer. He called that part of the hard drive the "server," since it "served" the web pages on demand to the web browser. He wrote another software program that instructed the server to receive the messages from remote computers and to send along the desired pages.

When it was all put together, he finally had a working model of the World Wide Web. It was, for the moment, entirely on his own NeXT machine, but it was a complete system by December. The whole thing had taken less than three months of work.

In *Weaving the Web*, Tim describes how it was so easy for a genius to accomplish such a task in so short a time.

"What was often difficult for people to understand about the design was that there was nothing else beyond URIs, HTTP, and HTML," he explained. "There was no central computer 'controlling' the Web, no single network on which these protocols worked, not even an organization anywhere that 'ran' the Web. The Web was not a physical 'thing' that existed in a certain 'place.' It was the 'space' in which information existed."

Robert Cailliau was Tim Berners-Lee's friend. He was the first person to install Berners-Lee's World Wide Web software on another computer.

Chapter 6

The Web Spreads Around the World

• •

The first version of the World Wide Web was finished in December 1990. By Christmas, Robert Cailliau, a friend of Berners-Lee's at CERN, bought his own NeXT machine and installed all of the World Wide Web software on his machine. At this point the World Wide Web was still not much at all.

In May 1991, Paul Kunz from the Stanford University Linear Accelerator Program returned to Stanford from CERN and brought the World Wide Web back with him on his NeXT computer. Kunz gave the web software to Louise Addis, the librarian at the Linear Accelerator Program. She saw the vast potential of the Web to spread information to a global audience and helped to create the first web server outside of CERN to give real meaning to the term "World Wide Web." Soon other friends of the Web were establishing computer hard drives as servers to store and send information on a variety of subjects, from cooking recipes to rocket secrets.

There was still little information available and a NeXT machine was essential in order to use it. Nicola Pellow was a young English mathematics student who was working at CERN at the time. She was given the task of writing the computer software for a web browser, or client program, that could be used on any machine. Berners-Lee soon expanded the scope of the Web by having the browser be able to follow links to material sent by FTP and NNTS protocols. Quickly the World Wide Web could display all of the material on the Internet. Many of the scientific community that had used the Internet liked the speed of HTTP and the ability of the World Wide Web.

Berners-Lee and Cailliau began spending a lot of time at computer and scientific conferences showing the World Wide Web in action. They petitioned others to join the World Wide Web, to create databases of hypertext pages and store them on servers of their own. That was all it took to join. By using HTTP to tell a remote server to send a HTML document that was identified by an URI over packets controlled by TCP/IP, anyone could join the World Wide Web. Between the summers of 1991 and 1994, the number of people who chose to view the information Berners-Lee had posted on the first Web server rose steadily by a factor of 10 every year. By 1994, there were over 100,000 different computers around the world using the World Wide Web.

Then Tim Berners-Lee did something that was truly inspired and perhaps great. In 1993, he gave away all rights to URIs, HTTP, and HTML. He made the World Wide Web free for everyone all over the world. He had had a great insight. He knew that people would be happy to get something very valuable for nothing. If he had kept the rights to even one part of his World Wide Web, there would always be people who were unhappy and would try to invent another way to do it.

But by giving it away, Berners-Lee gave his wonderful new invention a virtually certain chance of becoming a success. He would receive no riches for it, but people would be happy to work together to make it better and better. He told Spencer Reiss of *Forbes* magazine, "If I didn't give it away, it wouldn't have happened."

The World Wide Web was quickly becoming more and more popular around the world. It rose from 100 communications in the summer of 1991, to 1,000 a day in the summer of 1992. The rapid development of better and more capable web browsers was the single most important factor in the increased general popularity of the Web. The Web had always been able to transmit any kind of digital information in its TCP/IP packets. Not only text, but music, pictures and even other computer programs can be sent. HTML was the kind of a language that easily put graphics on the screen.

The hard part was to write the software for the web client, the program that displayed these pictures and sounds of the World Wide Web to its user. In 1993, Marc Andreessen and his friends who were working for the National Center for Supercomputing Applications, or NCSA, at the University of Illinois built the Mosaic Web browser.

The Mosaic browser was just what the vast potential audience for the World Wide Web wanted. It could display full-color graphics within its display window and it had numerous controls available to the user. It had different fonts. Besides this, Marc Andreessen and his associates soon released a product called Navigator 1.0 that was able to work on the most popular computers found in the homes of the world: the PC that ran on the Microsoft Corporation operating system, and the MacIntosh that employed the Apple Corporation operating system. They also gave the Netscape 1.0 browser away for free.

Once this was accomplished, the World Wide Web quickly spread to the homes and families of the world. Everyone found a use for the Web. In 1993, the World Wide Web was used for over a million communications a day. Soon it was tens of millions a day. Then even more. Both of the most popular web browsers in current use are based on the original Mosaic browser.

In the 1990s, the World Wide Web gained popularity in homes and offices all around the world, thanks in large part to Berners-Lee's efforts to promote it.

Chapter 7

Legacy

● ●

Today Tim Berners-Lee is married to Nancy Carlson, an American whom he met at an acting workshop while she was working for the World Health Organization in Switzerland. They have two children and live close to the Massachusetts Institute of Technology, or MIT, where he now works.

At MIT, he directs the World Wide Web Consortium, or "W3C" as it is called. W3C has some 40 full time staff members and over 200 members, mostly companies who are interested in or make their money on the World Wide Web. Members pay to belong and are allowed to attend the meetings and conferences of the W3C. At these meetings, the W3C discusses problems, such as how to make business dealings secure and how to prevent unwarranted break-ins, called "hacking." The W3C also decides on new protocols that will be used on the World Wide Web. New versions of HTTP are examples of new and revised standards.

Being the head of the W3C is not a particularly well paying job, especially in the light of the hundreds of millions of dollars Berners-Lee could have made from his invention. It's not a particularly easy job either. There is always something changing on the web, and there are always several ideas that are often backed by large companies and their desires about what to do about those problems. Berners-Lee has to steer the W3C and ultimately the World Wide Web itself. Each company that becomes a member of W3C signs a contract that gives him the ultimate power to make the decisions. But it's typical of Berners-Lee's personality that he has never just made a decision, but rather he always seeks to have others agree.

Carl Cargill of Netscape Corp., one of the member companies, says in a profile of Berners-Lee appearing in *Scientific American*'s online site that "Tim doesn't work that way. Tim leads by his vision. And if you disagree with his vision, he will talk to you and talk to you until he agrees with your vision or you agree with his—or both of you come to a new vision."

Tim Berners-Lee has been honored by those around him who strive to honor excellence of mind. He has honorary degrees from the Parsons School of Design in New York, Southampton University, Essex University, Southern Cross University, and the Open University. He is a Distinguished Fellow of the British Computer Society, and an Honorary Fellow of the Institution of Electrical Engineers. In 1996 he was awarded the Order of the British Empire, so he now holds the title of "Sir Tim Berners-Lee." In 1999, *Time* magazine dubbed him one of the 100 greatest minds of the century.

Despite all these honors, he leads a very quiet life. He drives an old car and on his official website, in response to the question, "Can you tell me more about your personal life?" his answer is very simple: "No, I can't—sorry. I like to keep work and personal life separate."

Tim continues to work hard to keep up with the administration and progress of the World Wide Web. He is still vitally interested in the development of the Web as a tool for humans to use to solve their common problems. His vision is still compelling.

"You should write and read what you believe in," he said in the *Scientific American* interview. "And if you keep doing that, then you will create a Web that is one of value. If other people read it, then your ideas spread. But that is not a prerequisite. The Web doesn't force anything down your throat. If you are worried that your children are going to read low-quality information, teach them. Teach them what to read. Teach them how to judge information."

Tim Berners-Lee is a very private man with a great interest in the public good, which he hopes the World Wide Web will always serve.

Tim Berners-Lee Chronology

- 1955, born in London, England on June 8.
- 1961, starts school.
- 1969, enrolls in a private high school, the Emanuel School.
- 1973, graduates from Emanuel and enrolls at Oxford University, one of the oldest and best universities in the world. While at college, builds his first computer.
- 1976, graduates from Oxford with first-class honors in theoretical physics, then goes to work for the Plessey Telecommunications Company in Dorset, England.
- 1978, leaves his job at Plessey and goes to work for the D. G. Nash company, where he designs computer programs for typesetting machines, used for printing books.
- 1980, begins work with the European Laboratory for Particle Physics, known as CERN (its name in French is *Centre Européen de Recherche Nucléaire*), where he develops a database to keep track of the many people he met as part of his job. It uses hypertext to link records.
- 1981-1984, works at John Poole's Image Computer Systems Ltd., then returns to CERN.
- 1989, after learning about an American computer network called the Internet, begins work to improve upon the idea.
- 1990, finishes first version of the World Wide Web in December.
- 1991, gives copy of World Wide Web software to an American physicist returning to the United States from a stint at CERN, after which it gradually begins to spread.
- 1993, declares he will not keep the rights to URIs, HTTP, and HTML, all of which he has designed for the Web.
- 1994, joins Laboratory for Computer Science (LCS) at the Massachusetts Institute of Technology (MIT).
- 1999, becomes the first holder of the 3Com Founders chair at MIT.
- 2001, directs World Wide Web Consortium, which coordinates Web developments world-wide and seeks to realize full potential of the Web.

World Wide Web Timeline

- **1945**: World War II ends and the Cold War begins, during which the United States and the Soviet Union stand on the brink of nuclear war, ever ready to launch atomic weapons at each other.

- **1957**: The Soviet Union launches Sputnik, the first satellite, into outer space. The US government, fearing the use of satellites in atomic warfare, decides to create plans to protect the most important scientific and military people and information in case of such an attack.

- **1969**: To move data from one government computer to another, the Advanced Research Projects Agency (ARPA), part of the Defense Department, officially grants funds to build a network of scientific computers called ARPANET.

- **1973**: The ARPANET network expands to include satellites and packet radio. Then a new system is needed to send information between machines. Vinton Cerf and Robert Kahn, employees of ARPA, invent a way to separate messages in packets.

- **1977**: The first message is sent using Transmission Control Protocol, or TCP, the packet system. A message was sent from San Francisco, California to London, England and then back to the University of Southern California using SATNET, radio packets, and the ARPANET. Not one bit of information is lost.

- **1978**: The packet system improves when Internet Protocol (IP) is invented. It is used to address a packet and make sure that all of it arrives at its destination.

- **1980s**: More and more universities begin to take part in ARPANET and it begins to be referred to as the Internet. The name ARPANET goes out of use. E-mail begins.

- **1983**: Beginning in 1983, TCP/IP gradually starts to be used by all computer systems for network communication.

- **1989**: The Defense Department ceases to use ARPANET. But the Internet lives on, as universities and many other institutions remain linked via computers.
- **1990**: Tim Berners-Lee develops idea for World Wide Web software on his own computer.
- **1991**: Over the summer, 100 communications are made over the World Wide Web.
- **1992**: World Wide Web communications are made at the rate of one thousand per day by the summer.
- **1993**: Berners-Lee decides to give all rights to URIs, HTTP, and HTML away to the world for free. Nobody ever pays a charge to him to use his inventions when they put up a Web page. The World Wide Web begins to grow wildly in terms of popularity.
- **1994**: More than 100,000 different computers around the world use the World Wide Web.
- **2001**: Hundreds of millions of computers around the world use the World Wide Web, which seems guaranteed only to grow in importance.

Further Reading

Berners-Lee, Tim with Mark Fischetti. *Weaving the Web.* San Francisco: HarperSanFrancisco, 1999.

Cook, Peter and Scott Manning. *Why Doesn't My Floppy Disk Flop.* New York: John E. Wiley & Sons, 2000.

"Interview with Tim Berners-Lee," World Wide Web Journal, posted on the Web at http://www.oreilly.com/www/info/wj/issue3/tbl-int.html.

"Interviews with Visionaries: Tim Berners-Lee, Inventor, World Wide Web," posted on Intel's home page at http://www.intel.com/intel/museum/25anniv/int/berner.htm#first.

Jefferis, David. *Cyber Space: Virtual Reality and the World Wide Web.* New York: Crabtree, 1999.

Oxland, Chris. *Communication Through Time.* Austin, Texas: Raintree Steck Vaughn, 1996.

"Molding the Web" [profile of Tim Berners-Lee], posted on Scientific American's Web page at http://www.sciam.com/1297issue/1297profile.html.

Pedersen, Ted. *Make Your Own Web Page: A Guide for Kids.* New York: Price Stern Sloan, 1998.

Quittner, Joshua. "Tim Berners-Lee," *Time*, vol. 153, no. 12 (March 29, 1999).

Stewart, Melissa. *Tim Berners-Lee: Inventor of the World Wide Web.* Chicago, IL: Ferguson Publishing Co., 2001.

"Tim Berners-Lee, Short Biography." Posted on the World Wide Web Consortium's site at http://www.w3org/People/Berners-Lee/ShortHistory.html

Wright, Robert. "The Man who Invented the Web," *Time*, v. 149 (May 19, 1997)

Glossary of Terms

communications - the act of sending and receiving messages; today people have many means of communications, including telephones and computers.

database - a collection of data designed so it can easily be searched.

Domain Name System - system under which Web sites' names are assigned, with .com, .org, .net, etc., at the end.

gateway - something that serves as a means of access, or a way in.

HTML - Hypertext Mark-Up Language, a fully functional word processing program that allows the creation, browsing, and editing of hypertext pages.

HTTP - Hypertext Transfer Protocol, a computer software program that packages hypertext pages into a form that the packets of TCP/IP can deliver between machines and then reconstruct into machine-readable HTML form.

hypertext - system by which text on a Web page is highlighted or underlined, indicating that if it is clicked upon it will take the user to a link, or related page.

IP - Internet Protocol, the procedure that addresses packets as they are sent over telephone lines between computers and makes sure that all packets—parts of a message—arrive.

link - connecting element.

military - relating to the armed forces (the navy, army, air force and marines).

multitask - to perform several functions at once.

network - when used in terms of computers, a system that links computers by telephone wires so they can share information.

nuclear war - a war fought with nuclear weapons, which contain are extremely dangerous

packet - a small bundle of information.

physics - branch of science that deals with matter and energy, and interaction between the two.

programs - set of instructions that tell a computer what to do to perform a specific task.

programmer - person who writes computer programs.

protocol - when used in connection with computers, a standard procedure for regulating data transmission between machines.

satellite - object that is launched from earth into outer space and orbits the planet.

TCP - Transmission Control Protocol, the procedure that splits a message being sent from one computer to another over a telephone line into packets.

URI - Universal Resource Identifier, the address the computer points to when a darkened hypertext link is chosen by the user.

Index